How to Go From Soul Mates to Roommates in 10 Easy Steps

By Caroline Madden, MFT

TRAIN OF THOUGHT
PRESS

Publisher's Note

This book is designed to provide information and motivation to our readers. It is sold with the understanding that the publisher is not engaged to render any type of psychological, legal, or any other kind of professional advice. No warranties or guarantees are expressed or implied by the publisher's choice to include any of the content in this volume. No therapeutic relationship is established. Neither the publisher nor the individual author shall be liable for any physical, psychological, emotional, financial, or commercial damages, including, but not limited to, special, incidental, consequential, or other damages. Our views and rights are the same: You are responsible for your own choices, actions, and results.

ISBN-10: 0990772810
ISBN-13: 978-0-9907728-1-1

Summary: A tongue-in-cheek guide to preserve the spark in your marriage.

Connie Johnston
Train of Thought Press
2275 Huntington Drive, #306
San Marino, CA 91108
Connie@TrainofThoughtPress.com
www.TrainOfThoughtPress.com

Dedication

This book is dedicated to my parents, Bill & Irene Madden, who showed throughout their 44 years together what a loving marriage could and should be. When asked what the secret to a long marriage is, they would say, "Trust and a sense of humor." Dad, you are missed.

Acknowledgments

I owe a debt of gratitude to both Dr. Samantha Rodman (aka Dr. Psych Mom) and Rachel Mork for their professional advice and assistance in polishing this manuscript.

And, of course, I would like to thank my own spouse of over 15 years, MT. It isn't easy being married to a therapist!

Author's Note

The first half of this book is written tongue-in-cheek. As a relationship therapist, I've found that it is sometimes easier to talk about touchy subjects if discussed with humor. The second half of this book is written in a more serious tone, but the entire piece delivers tried and true advice for protecting and enhancing your marriage.

Contents

Do you want to ruin a perfectly good relationship? Drive your spouse into a lover's arms? This is easier to accomplish than you may think.

Just follow these 10 simple steps:

Step One: Be too busy to connect.

Start in the morning. There's no better way to let your partner know you don't care than by starting the day being negative and critical. Early morning cuddling? Forget it! How about serving up an omelet of criticism with a dash of spicy neglect? This will definitely leave your spouse feeling resentful towards you all day long.

Not sure if you're up to the task? Here are some easy tips to get you started:

- Sleep in later than your spouse does each morning. Or complain and sulk about getting woken up.
- Make only enough coffee for you. Drink every last drop. For bonus points, leave them the mug to wash.
- Turn your cheek to your spouse when he or she goes in for a kiss. Gold star if you complain about bad breath.

Bonus Tip: Ignore text messages during the day or reply hours later with a terse response. Make it clear that work is far more important than anything your spouse might want to tell you.

1

Step Two: Overwhelm your spouse the second he or she walks through the door.

You know how weary your partner is at the end of the workday? Then obviously you realize it's the perfect time to ambush your spouse with problems and questions, making him or her want to turn around and go back out – anywhere but home.

After a hard day of work, be sure to:
- Slam the pots and pans around as you make dinner and complain about your day. Make it clear that your day was harder than your spouse's day possibly could have been.
- Make sure you describe your day in the most negative and dire terms possible. For a challenge, find a creative way to blame your spouse for the worst of it.
- As you walk in the door, say something negative before even saying "hello".
- Grumble under your breath about household tasks as you do them. But, and this is key: Accept no help.

Bonus Tip: If your spouse does help, criticize his or her efforts. Get personal; make jabs that you are sure will both pierce and demoralize your partner.

Step Three: Turn family dinner into a business meeting.

You know your spouse really just wants to relax and enjoy some time with you, so fill the evening with a never-ending list of demands. Make it unpleasant by doing the following:

- List all the things you want your spouse to do while you are eating dinner. Complain that he or she hasn't done them yet. Bonus points if you shrilly ask, "Are you listening?" when your spouse's mouth is too full to answer.
- Busy yourself with electronics as you "listen" to your spouse talk about the day. The best way to show you're present is to murmur "Uh, huh... uh, huh..." and nod at random intervals that are unrelated to what was just said.
- Leave the TV on while you eat. Don't talk. Make it clear that other people's fictional lives are more interesting than the real life of your partner.
- If you aren't good at ruining dinner conversations, eat dinner without your spouse. Forget to save any extra for your spouse.

Bonus Tip: Leave the dirty dishes on the table. You had a rough day, remember?

Step Four: Stop caring about your appearance.

Your spouse promised to be faithful to you no matter what, right? Test this by letting your appearance go. Try the following tried and true strategies:

- Gain weight, and use it as a reason to not be physically intimate, but don't do anything about it. Just complain.
- Stop showering or basic grooming. Save water by not shaving your legs.
- Wear the same sweatpants at home every day. That pair from college.
- Refuse to buy new clothes that flatter your body. Instead, hide in baggy clothing or squeeze into stuff that's too tight. You're not going to get new clothes until you lose those extra pounds. Your spouse should appreciate your commitment to principles, right?

Bonus Tip: Dress up only when going out with friends. Looking attractive is for strangers.

Step Five: Stop making special memories with your spouse.

Special memories act like relationship glue, but you don't want any of that sticky mushy gushy stuff. Push your spouse away by doing the following:

- Pour your energy entirely into the kids and their needs each evening. Better yet, leave your spouse to deal with the kids while you hole up in the office watching Netflix. Remind your spouse that you need some down time if he or she complains.
- Always invite other people out with you--the more the merrier! Extra points if you later compare other relationships to yours with phrases like, "Did you see how he looked at her? I can't remember the last time you looked at me that way."
- Reject your spouse's suggestion of a romantic date. Dates are for people who are dating, not married.

Bonus Tip: When walking, walk a couple of steps ahead of your spouse. Or a couple of blocks.

Step Six: Never say, "I love you."

Your spouse doesn't need to be complimented. You thought enough of them to get married, didn't you? Criticizing your spouse is a great way to grow apart. Try the following:

- Comment on clothing only when negative, like to mention that something doesn't fit right or is unflattering.
- Joke about your spouse's appearance, especially things you know he or she is self-conscious about. Bonus points if you mock your wife's baby weight and the baby isn't yet crawling.
- If you have something negative to say, don't say it privately. Criticize your spouse in front of other people. Wait until there is a big enough audience so everyone can laugh. And by "laugh" I mean feel incredibly uncomfortable.

Bonus Tip: You said, "I love you" once. Any more and it loses its value.

Step Seven: Don't go to bed together.

Stay up later than your spouse or go to bed significantly earlier. Make it clear that you don't care if you get time to snuggle or talk in bed before falling asleep – that kind of intimacy is for sissies.

If you really want to hurt the relationship, do the following:

- Stay up after your spouse goes to bed playing around on the computer. Let your spouse wonder if you're looking at porn or emailing with an ex-girlfriend through Facebook. Better yet, leave the porn up on the computer screen for her to find in the morning. Maybe seeing those women will be the motivation she needs to drop some weight!
- Go to bed earlier than your spouse, complaining that you never get enough sleep. Make it clear that sex is out of the question. Snore.
- Leave the lights or TV on while your spouse is trying to sleep.

Bonus Tip: If your spouse asks you to go to bed at the same time, sigh loudly and explain that you need a little time alone once in a while. Make it obvious that you find the request to be burdensome and unappealing.

Step Eight: Demand that your spouse meets all your needs.

Criticize your spouse for falling short in any way. Make it clear that you expect your spouse to be perfect, and, while at it, that your spouse should read your mind and always know what you need.

To perfect this step, you will want to:

- Allow yourself to feel upset when your spouse doesn't "get" an interest of yours. Sulk about it. Stop doing anything your partner doesn't like and be sure to tell anyone who will listen: "My spouse won't let me do it." Sigh.
- Demand your spouse likes everything you do. When he or she doesn't like something, magnify this in your mind, telling yourself you are incompatible. "If we were soul mates, he would enjoy watching design shows on HGTV..."
- Don't go to anything that you don't want to do just because it is important to your spouse. If you do begrudgingly go, be sure to mope in the corner. Don't talk to anyone, and make it clear that your partner should babysit you.

Bonus Tip: Get really angry after your spouse doesn't attend a function with you. (Pretend you're okay at first, but get upset after the fact, when nothing can be changed.) Then refuse to accept your spouse's excuse, no matter how valid. Bring this up whenever you start to lose an argument. It's your new trump card – use it!

Step Nine: Use sex as a weapon. (Otherwise known as "the great bait and switch tactic".)

Who needs sex anymore? Sex is for newlyweds. Surely your spouse can't expect you to put out after a long day's work or a demanding day with the kids.

To drive this point home, make sure you:
- Roll your eyes and groan when your spouse initiates. Better yet, bat his or her hand away and complain that you hate being groped. If possible, make your spouse feel ashamed.
- Be too tired for sex. If that isn't working, claim you have a headache. Or a backache. Or your period (even if you are a man). Whatever works to keep your spouse away.
- Agree to sex, but only right before bed, under the covers, with the lights off. Same position every time.
- Let your spouse do all the "work". Don't let him think you are actually enjoying it and connecting with the experience. After all, he's lucky he's getting anything at all. Be sure to use phrases like "Hurry Up" and "Are you done yet?" You get a gold star if you can fall asleep before he's finished.

Bonus Tip: Make it clear that you expect complete fidelity even though you aren't interested in sex.

Step Ten: Blame your spouse for anything that's wrong in the relationship.

None of this "turning into roommates" stuff could possibly be your fault, right? Make sure your spouse knows you are blameless and turn it into a finger-pointing match by doing the following:

- Note the negatives and not the positives.
- Refuse to apologize for anything or to hear your spouse's side.
- Don't tell your spouse when you're upset; just assume the worst and let the anger fester instead of finding solutions together. Assume no solutions are even possible. Tell him or her this, frequently.
- Get depressed about the sad state of your relationship and feel bad for yourself. Don't get help or seek counseling. Counseling is for couples who both have problems. Here, it's all your spouse.
- Surround yourself with people who agree that your marital problems are all your spouse's fault. Extra points if some of these are mutual friends that can then judge your spouse when you're all out together.

Bonus Tip: Keep score. Foster a you-versus-me mentality.

If you follow these 10 easy steps, you will feel like strangers in no time!

On a Serious Note…

For Those Who Want to Affair-Proof a Marriage Instead of Tank It

Although there are some people that will jump into an affair no matter what you do, most couples I see in my office for affair recovery are there because the real connection between the spouses has ended. This lack of connection made the relationship vulnerable to an affair.

The relationship has usually become transactional, meaning the communication has deteriorated into talk about what needs to be done, and, of course, criticism for everything on the to-do list that hasn't gotten done. Couples say, "I love you" out of habit instead of passion, and have boring sex (if they have sex at all). Connecting on a soulful level has stopped. When you lose the emotional connection, you make the relationship vulnerable to threats from the outside.

The following steps are ways I recommend that couples restructure their lives to ensure their soul mate connection doesn't devolve into living like roommates.

Step One: Develop morning rituals that remind you to connect.

How do you usually say good morning? Create a ritual that you find bonding. For example, you could do one of the following:

- Set the coffee maker the night before, and then go pour each of you a cup of coffee first thing in the morning. Deliver it with a kiss.
- Make breakfast for you both to eat together. Five minutes of togetherness each morning will start the day off right.
- Text a daily "Good morning, I hope you have a good day today" message every morning before you start work. Personalize the message whenever possible. For example, text "I'm sure you will knock that presentation out of the park" or "Hope that meeting goes well." Extra credit if you text something sexy to the spouse who is always angling for more physical affection.
- When you leave in the morning, give your spouse a real kiss. Not just a peck on the cheek.
- Create a ritual that works for you and your spouse, something that is uniquely yours.

Bonus Tip: If your spouse gets up before you because you are a stay-at-home parent, are self-employed and working from home, or are unemployed, make it a point at least once every other week to get up (as in out of bed) and make the coffee/breakfast. Better yet, join your spouse in the shower. Why? Because even the most enlightened, loving spouse becomes resentful of leaving in the morning to go to work while the other spouse is sleeping in. Also, it is a good reminder for you as to how difficult it is to get up and go to work. It will make you think twice before starting a difficult conversation or fight right bedtime if you also have to get up early.

Step Two: Make your home into an oasis.

You need to think of your home as a sacred oasis, a place where the both of you can relax, connect and get your needs met in peace and harmony.

I'm not saying you should ignore the practical demands of life, and I know it's important that partners feel able to freely complain about life struggles. However, you will need to learn how to commiserate supportively instead of bitch about problems in ways that burden your spouse.

The following are strategies for making your home a safe, harmonious place where you both feel rejuvenated instead of drained or stressed:

- Be the first to greet your spouse when he or she walks in the door. (Yes, before the kids. It's good for them to see that you prioritize your marriage, that husbands and wives welcome each other and miss each other.) Put a smile on your face, give a hug, and say, "Welcome home. How was your day?"
- Do something that you both find relaxing (together) each night. You may want to cuddle, watch TV, play a game, go for a walk, listen to music, read, or engage in a hobby or sport you both enjoy. Whatever it is, do something that you both enjoy, and do it together.
- Come up with a plan for discussing issues that need to be delegated or complaints. Reserve a certain day and time each week to deal with these

issues instead of daily dumping on each other. Make your usual routine be one of expressing support and relaxing together instead of talking about stressful topics.

Step Three: Talk during dinner.

Turn of all electronics while you have dinner and use this time to talk about the day and truly connect. Try to have conversations about something other than all the things that need to be done and events that need to be planned. Have a moment where you concentrate on the present and how lucky you both are to have found each other.

The following strategies will improve your dinners together:

- Be honest with yourself about dinner plans. Are you both burnt out on cooking? Invest money into bringing home take out, ordering in, or making meals on the weekend that can be easily reheated during the week. The investment will relieve you both of this burden and make it easier to relax during dinner.
- Refuse to complain about anything that might stress your spouse until you've had time to connect emotionally. Then, when venting, make it clear that you don't expect your spouse to fix the problem, but that you just need to talk about the stresses of the day.
- Be actively supportive as your spouse talks about the day. Listen carefully, and ask thoughtful questions. Sympathize. Touch.
- Say encouraging things that you truly mean. As your spouse tells you about the events of the day, think of the things you admire about your spouse, and find ways to express these things verbally.

Step Four: Care about your appearance and overall grooming.

Alrighty, wives, let's talk. In the beginning of your relationship you didn't hang out in sweatpants all day. I get the fact that having small kids is tough, and I'm not saying that you should put on pearls and lipstick. But ask yourself this: Would you wear what you are wearing if someone else were coming to your house?

And men: Shower. Groom. Brush your teeth. *Manscape.* For bonus points, get rid of the T-shirts with holes in them.

I'm not saying you need to look polished every minute of the day, but it's important that you invest time in your appearance on a regular basis. If you feel pressed for time, try the following tips:

- Get a haircut that is easy to style or naturally lies nicely so you don't have to spend gobs of time on your hair.
- When you find an item of clothing that is particularly flattering, buy a couple of them in different colors.
- Invest in a wardrobe that you can mix and match easily so you always have something to throw on that looks good (without requiring much thought or effort.)

Step Five: Schedule a regular date night.

You need to make time to connect on a romantic level. A romantic partnership is the foundation of a stable loving family. Try to let go of any guilt you may be feeling about spending time and/or money on yourselves. Remember, creating a stable family structure outweighs any short-term discomfort your child (or you!) may have.

The goal of date night is to feel connected to your partner as a human being again and not just relate to each other as co-parents/co-CEOs of the family. Choose a night each week (or every other week) to go out, just the two of you. Get a sitter and go do something together that you both enjoy.

Allow yourself to transition from "Mommy" and "Daddy" to wife and husband. On the date, do your best to be present mentally. Do not check email or "check-in" on Facebook. Only answer calls from the babysitter.

A word to Husbands:
The goal of date night is to help your wife to remember why she married you in the first place. She might have a hard time transitioning from mommy to wife. Reassure her in a positive way that she is allowed to be a human being too.

Do things you used to do when you were dating. Compliment her on how she looks. Touch her. Put your arm around her and hold her hand. Act like the guys in the movies she always wants you to watch with her.

Please do not use date night just to get sex. Often, women complain to me that her partner won't do anything romantic unless he is hoping to get lucky. This then ruins it for her and she feels like she has been manipulated. Sometimes the entire evening can overwhelm a woman, but she feels connected to you and is more interested in sex the night after, or the night after that.

A word to Wives:
No, the night doesn't have to end in sex. But, as you need to connect *emotionally* through words, most men need to connect *physically* to feel close.

Women tend to boil down physical intimacy to the physical act of sex. Understand that for men, it is a whole lot more than just an orgasm. Making love to you is the way he feels that he is valued, that he is special, and that you still view him as "your man". Male clients have told me that sex with their wife makes them feel less like a "walking ATM machine" that "can't ever do anything right" and more like part of a team, and therefore, willing to do more to help the partnership.

To put it in female terms:
How would you feel if after a night of having sex, he didn't talk to you? That's how he feels if he spends the evening romancing you and you don't make love. If

you're exhausted, it doesn't have to be a two-hour session. It can be a fairly quick but still loving encounter. Just don't tell him to hurry up!

Step Six: Compliment your spouse.

Your spouse needs to feel admired, adored and respected. That means you need to make a conscious effort to compliment your spouse. Notice the things your partner has done, recognize and verbally appreciate them.

Try the following:

- Give specific compliments. Saying "You look pretty" is good; saying "That dress brings out your gorgeous eyes" is better. Likewise, saying, "Thanks for staining the deck" is good; saying, "The deck looks fabulous – thank you for working so hard in the blazing sun all day" is better.
- For every one negative interaction, aim for 5 (Yes, 5!) positive comments.
- Let your spouse catch you saying something nice behind his or her back. Bonus points if they overhear you complimenting them while talking to someone they really respect.
- Learn to accept compliments. When your spouse says you look beautiful/handsome say "thank you" and smile.

Step Seven: Try to go to bed at the same time.

Going to sleep is as important as starting the day off right. If you go to bed separately, you risk feelings of loneliness or feeling disconnected. Some of the best conversations and experiences can happen in that precious time just before falling asleep; we are at our most vulnerable in those moments of comfortable snuggling or relaxation.

The following suggestions can help make this a special time:

- Switch off the TV so that you aren't going to sleep with it on.
- Give each other a kiss and hold hands before turning over.
- Snuggle, spoon or give a back rub as you relax in bed together.
- Share a story from the day or positive sentiment before you fall asleep.

Step Eight: Accept that one person can't give you everything you need.

Cultivate your friendships and encourage your spouse to do the same. It takes the pressure off the marriage to be everything each other. Just make sure you choose healthy relationships that enhance your marriage instead of detract from it. Try the following:

- Make time for a good friend or group activity that feeds your soul at least once a month, if not once a week.
- Find something you and your spouse like to do together but also opens you up to building new relationships, like going out to dinner with another couple, playing cards with other couples, or joining a group activity together (tennis league, running club, sports team, etc.)
- Ask your spouse about his or her interests. Remember how exciting it was way back in the beginning of the relationship, when you actually liked finding out what made your lover tick? Remind yourself that your differences are what make the relationship interesting.

Step Nine: Make regular sex a priority.

Connecting sexually will help you connect emotionally. Try the following tips to keep your spouse sexually satisfied and feeling both loved and valued:

- Look forward to connecting with each other romantically. Avoid "tic tock" sex – you know, sex where you are just going through the motions, but aren't connecting to the experience.
- If you are avoiding sex because of something you want (or don't want) your spouse to do sexually, say it! Believe me, your spouse would rather know that there is something they can fix instead of feeling crappy that their spouse always rejects them.
- Ask your spouse how often he or she would like to make love. At least then you know what your partner is hoping for. When they act disconnected, you will know that it is because they haven't felt their needs are being met.
- Talk to your spouse about what makes sex good for you. If you need to connect emotionally before having sex, explain what that means for you and what your spouse can do to make that connection happen. Give concrete suggestions.

Important: If you don't have a high libido and this is causing problems in your marriage, get help from a professional therapist. You will be surprised at how much progress can be made if you just open up to someone who is trained in this area.

You cannot expect that your partner will just learn to deal with your low libido. The idea that if something isn't important to you it can't possibly be a big deal to your partner is just wrong. This idea shows a marked lack of perspective taking. Lack of affection, physical and otherwise, makes your partner feel unloved and unappreciated. It is those feelings that leave the relationship vulnerable to an affair and divorce.

Step Ten: Remember that you are on the same team.

As you deal with daily issues, focus on solving a problem rather than venting your anger or winning a victory.

It is as simple as this: You're either BOTH winning or you're BOTH losing. When you have "won" it means that your partner has "lost" and may feel like a "loser". Your partner is left feeling hurt, wounded, and unlovable. This doesn't lead to trust and intimacy. It leads to playing a game of who can find fault in the other first. Next time you may find that you are the "loser".

You can keep yourselves on the same team by doing the following:

- Assume that your partner is not purposely doing something to frustrate you, undermine you or control you. Instead, remind yourself that, "My partner loves me. S/he is a different person than I am. Why don't I ask how he or she views this situation?"
- Instead of assuming the worst and getting angry, ask questions.
- Give your spouse the benefit of the doubt. When you are temped to get angry (but don't yet know all the facts), tell yourself, "I'm sure there's a good reason behind this. I just don't know all the details yet."

- Tell your spouse that you want to understand. Then ask questions, listen to the answers with an open mind and explore potential solutions.

Soul Mates, Not Roommates

If you implement the strategies outlined in these ten steps, you can preserve the emotional connection that can help enhance your marriage. You'll grow closer, enjoy your relationship more and experience a deeper level of commitment.

Author Bio:

Caroline Madden, is a Pro-Marriage Therapist who specializes in Affair Recovery. She helps adult clients figure out how to build deeper, more satisfying relationships. Ms. Madden has been married for over a decade and has two young sons. For more information, please visit her author website: CarolineMadden.com.

Would you like a FREE eBook?

I hope you enjoyed *How to Go From Soul Mates to Roommates in 10 Easy Steps.* To thank you for ordering this book, I'd like to send you my next relationship eBook FREE.

Please visit my publisher at: TrainofThoughtPress.com to pre-order your free eBook.

For more relationship tips and advice, please visit my therapy website: CounselingWithCaroline.com.

Wishing You & Your Soul Mate the Best,

Caroline Madden, Marriage & Family Therapist

Made in the USA
San Bernardino, CA
19 December 2015